THOSE AMAZINGLY USEFUL EARS

Shirley Frederick
Illustrated with Photographs
Additional Illustrations by Ka Botzis

HAMPTON-BROWN

Some ears are big. Others are not.

Some ears are tall. Others are not.

Some ears are round. Others are not.

2

Ears can be amazingly different. In this book you will read about all kinds of ears— animal ears and human ears. You will see that people and animals are listeners. They use their ears to live fully and safely in their worlds.

People use their ears to listen to the world around them. With your ears you can hear what other people say. You can listen to great sounds, such as music. Your ears also help you hear loud sounds that tell you to avoid danger. Ears are hard workers.

Your ears
can listen even when you
are sleeping. For example, this
boy is a deep sleeper. At first, he did
not know that there was a storm outside.
He did not wake up when the lightning flashed
brightly. Then he heard the loud clap of thunder.

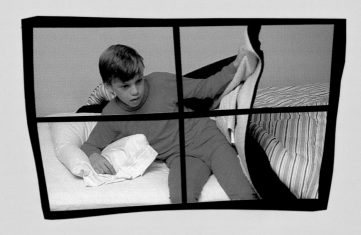

Sound travels in the air as waves. The light from the storm, called lightning, travels more rapidly than the sound, or thunder. That is why you hear the thunder after you see the lightning.

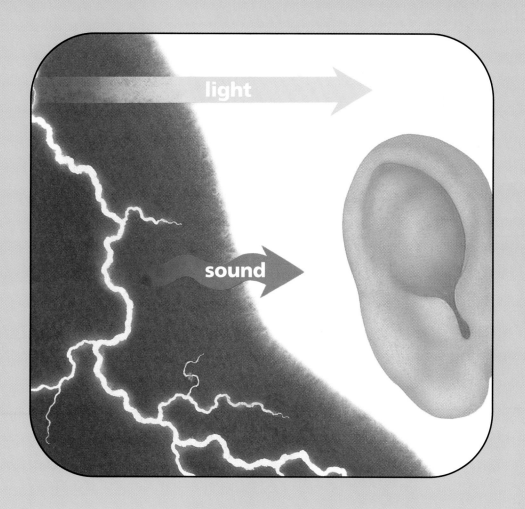

When a friend calls out your name, sound waves travel through the air. They arrive at your ears and move along the ear canal to the eardrum.

The sound waves make your eardrum move back and forth, or *vibrate*. A high sound makes your eardrum vibrate quickly. A low sound makes it vibrate more slowly.

The vibrations go from your eardrum to the small bones of your middle ear and then to your inner ear, deep inside your head. Your inner ear then turns the vibrations into signals that go to the brain.

Your Ear

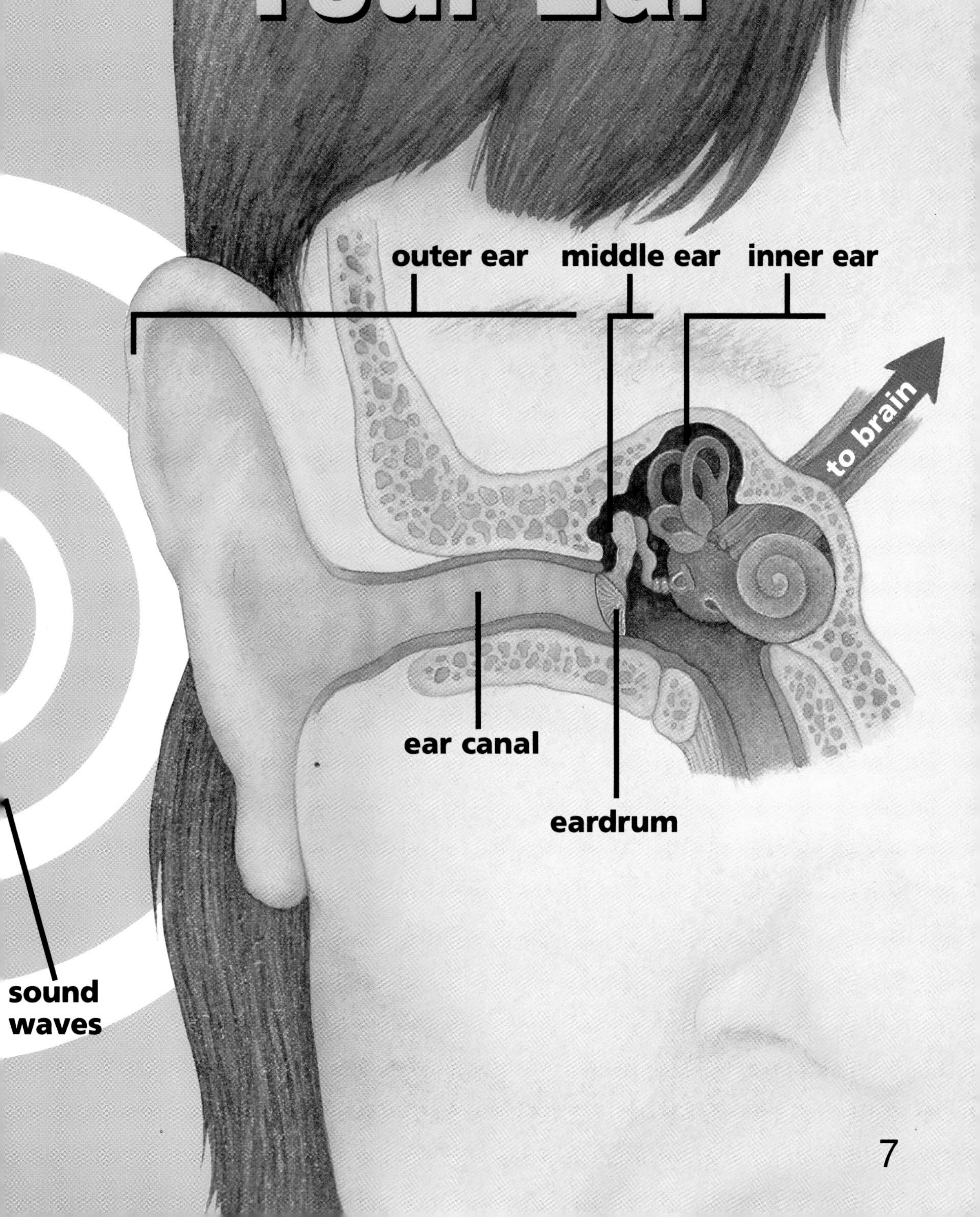

outer ear   middle ear   inner ear

to brain

ear canal

eardrum

sound
waves

Like people, animals use their ears in many different ways. Dogs, for example, have good ears. When a dog is listening hard, it perks up both of its ears. A dog can hear clearly many sounds that are too high for your ears to hear. In fact, a sound that you can hardly hear may seem loud to a dog.

Rabbits also hear very well. They can move both ears together or one at a time to hear sounds all around them. Rabbits are also fast runners. Their ears and legs help them escape from wolves and other animals who want to eat them.

The rabbit also uses its ears to keep cool on hot summer days. Its blood carries the heat from its body up into its ears, and then the heat goes into the air. In the winter the rabbit lays its ears on its back to keep the heat in.

Some birds are good singers. They sing so sweetly! Of course, other birds just screech loudly. The sounds may be different, but birds can still hear each other clearly— even though the ears on both sides of a bird's head are completely hidden by feathers!

The feathers on this owl's head help sounds go to both of its ears. The owl sits high in a tree and listens for animal sounds. It can hear a mouse move quietly in the leaves below. At night this hunter can quickly find the mouse just by hearing it.

Bats are fast fliers and hear very well. A bat that eats insects uses its ears to find food. It makes high sounds that human ears can't hear. The sound waves travel rapidly in the air. The bat listens for the sound to bounce off an insect, then it flies quickly to the insect and eats it.

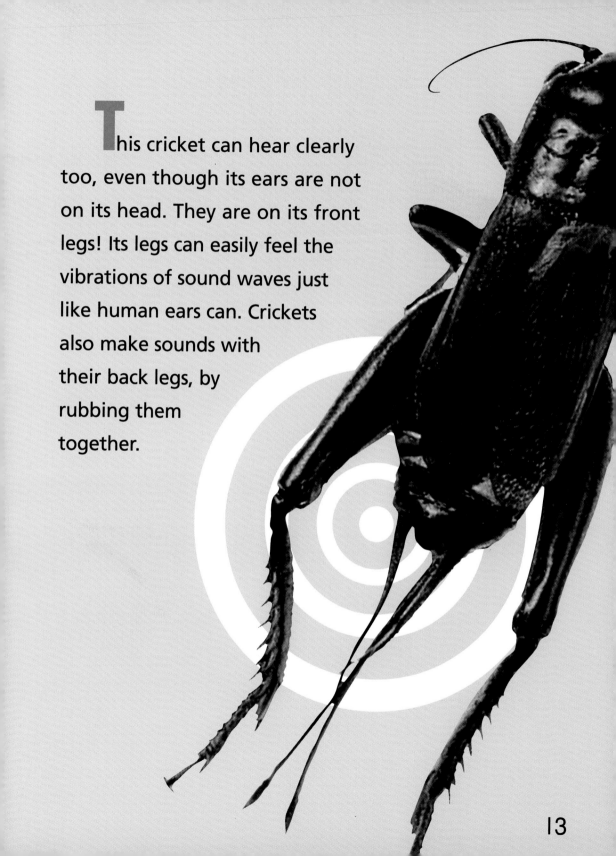

This cricket can hear clearly too, even though its ears are not on its head. They are on its front legs! Its legs can easily feel the vibrations of sound waves just like human ears can. Crickets also make sounds with their back legs, by rubbing them together.

This seal is a fast swimmer and a good diver. It has no outside ears. They would slow the seal down in the water. The seal *does* have little ear openings in its head, though. When it dives, both openings close completely so the water stays out. Even though their ears are shut, seals can hear extremely well under the water. They can hear many more sounds than people can.

Aren't ears amazing?

They come in many different shapes and sizes, but all types of ears help people and animals live fully and safely in their world. Let's hear it for ears!

THINK ABOUT IT

1. Tell how different animals use their ears.

2. Which animal do you think has the best ears? Why?

3. Be a good listener. What things in your classroom or home make sounds? What sounds do they make? Write a list.